THE BLOOD ABOUT THE HEART

the blood about the heart

By
Sarah
Menefee

CURBSTONE PRESS

Cover design by Pam Howard
Printed in the U.S.

Curbstone gratefully acknowledges the support of many individual
donors and The ADCO Foundation, The Bissell Foundation,
The Connecticut Commission on the Arts, The LEF Foundation,
The Lila Wallace-Reader's Digest Fund, The Andrew W. Mellon
Foundation, The National Endowment for the Arts, and
The Plumsock Fund,

Some of these poems have appeared in: *Acts, Beatitude, Conjunctions,
Deluge, Left Curve,* and *Queen of Heaven.*

ISBN: 0-915306-53-0
Library of Congress number: 91-58997

distributed by
InBook
Box 120261
East Haven, CT 06512

published by
CURBSTONE PRESS
321 Jackson Street
Willimantic, CT 06226

The Blood About the Heart

for just a moment I felt a flash of gratitude to my heart for beating all my life beyond my concern or thought

Empedocles: for the blood about the heart is human thought

the light of reflection is the one I'm desiring the light of the body
only conjectured from the face whose features are smudged in silver

I'm working night shift in a morgue. Feeling lonely, I open out a
drawer and start to talk to the two stiffs laying on it.

how long it takes for a glimmering of the world you who put the spine in my poem the dead of Jonestown knocking about our hearts and you unknown to me when the days got shorter in an autumn cloud you were releasing fierce words into the city

art drove me into the loony bin
standing shivering naked modeling for Montecito housewives
while the blood of a natural abortion gushed down my legs
sad bewildered paralyzed wanting to live a life of beauty
Picasso etchings the monster entrails of Guernica
grinning out from their mirrored bathroom walls

they stab me in the flank with a hypodermic needle I leap away in terror
hitting against bars it isn't cruelty they feel that they board me up
in darkness of crowded stalls in my own shit I'm all of them my suffering
multiplied utterly at the mercy of cold calculation till my heart can't
stand the pain on fading hooves I step away from the dream

when I was crazy for two weeks the hippy chick said I hid in a closet
but couldn't hide from the iron hooks that pulled my skin from my bones
I didn't bleed but suffered so much you can't imagine iron hooks two
weeks dying and every atom an eye that couldn't blink

in thanks for some coins in a rattling tin
and for signing declarations of war on Nixon's orgasm
she bakes us a Jonestown Passover cake
a lumpy thing with a toupee of icing and maraschino cherries
we keep three days on top of the cash register
then throw into the trash can outside the store
within five minutes somebody finds it there
and hurries it down the street the wind at his thin back

a palimpsest of all the times he walked by bearded flemish face and
a campy smile headband white panama red rag flapping at twilight red
sores on ankles of bare feet sticking out from a doorway his gracious
hello

maybe because I stand behind
a cash register all day long my fingers black
from tearing the carbons from charge card forms
but the corner I look on seems every day more sapped
of spirit a concrete weight on my mouth
so I can't cry out and I wonder if it's money
that makes even those who have some
walk with a malnourished twist of gait
clutching their heavy burdens of shopping bags

it lays on the surface like bought-out art
Van Gogh's sunflowers locked in a vault
that's why the lunatic voices are speaking to me
saying how in this mindless and broken state can any-
body be real

then late at night the sadness rises up an impersonal grief

Half a glass of red wine, embarrassing people in the bar with the weeping, and home in the rain, tears on my face again, over the hill on the bus. Far less drunk than last time. Oh god, here it comes again, it laughs and falls on my head.

I cried for a year inside, keeping the panic in as well as I could. About what? About the door of the heart that begins to open at thirty-five, in pain, with a breeze that blows through, and a cord of feeling that extends to the heart of another, and out into the spaces between the stars.

Looking up at the bare cheek of the moon. Oh what have we remembered: nothing but a face looking back down at the world. A sweet empty feeling, mingled delight and hunger.

All these years, knowing your hand would enter my mouth.

talk talk talk the black-lipped street woman said all day I talk my
asshole off

he used to be young and attractive not so long ago the sick boy hustler who goes by wrapped in a blanket that trails behind in the mud his bare feet cracked and indecent past groaning walls and gutters flowing with blood you on the corner with a plastic bag tied around your mouth we joke and laugh at the stiff-standing sight of you through the windows of our retail jobs today the jerking mumbling letters-to-the-police-chief crazy is wearing in his jacket lapel a full-blown rose summer's the unmistakable smell of roses in the hall that becomes fried fish behind a neighbor's door

I never was taught about hell when I was young but love the thought of
the earth's body-heat

smell that over loving years is a wide habitation

laying beside him so nice I leaned over and began to stroke his neck
a sweet suck of flesh down by the pulse of the throat

I love your loose-skinned body bitch

fuck-body my little suck-body go down after just any old cock

jasmine cocksucker he says that's what you are

I'll give you thick and deep

after he yelling comes I kiss a shoulder his shoulder I can't tell if it's his or mine my lips are touching

pressing my nose against his heart chakra

out of oblivion's black a knock on a door I open to a being I know is Revolution who stands there looking with red snake-eyes in red-scaled reptilian man-face with such fierce intelligence right through and beyond me

asked if I used to march in demonstrations in those days I said maybe
a little ways then was to be found upstairs in the Crossroads Lounge
or over in Oakland drinking with the sailors

a curb-by-the-fender life that's what it's become with no small patch
of relief for our twitching and broken walking and muttering

resting the eyes on a worn place an angry flame licking the rags of the
fallen

a loud guffawing man an entrepreneur has sold the Sphinx and the buyer
has taken it away so the salesman's saying in a hawhaw voice well
we're gonna have to replace it with another and sell that too

boys for sale leaning against the walls of boutiques I pass in the night
with aching breasts

a marriage proposal from a guy with a can held out for coins falling-down-drunk leading feeble-and-old

a man with matted hair stealing a sip of dregs from a cappuccino cup
in a rain of yells of get out get out I'll call the police get out

sometimes when I have a bottle you can stop and have a little his mother kneeling above three hotplates cooking Thanksgiving dinner at the end of time when time comes to an end there the faithful will be gathered together to dine on the great ham hocks of Leviathan's female

this light of September
the slant of shadows turning toward autumn
deadleaf brown the worn and streetgrimed clothes of the down-
at-heel cut off from the branch
and drifting

the I who enjoys the sight
of slatey mussels on a bed of ice
behind plate glass has been separated from
the one inside who looks out at the hungry
ones who all day drag themselves along
with hands stuck out like useless shameful things
shame on their faces and desperate want
and I'm ashamed of my blind aesthetic delight

from the patio of La Trattoria
a mingled smell of garlic and heavy perfumes
wafts to the corner can where a shrunken Charlton Heston
pokes the stick of his arm checking for anything edible
a shriek alarm goes off in an empty car

sometimes I hate this world
that gags me with a particular smell of apple blossoms
and urine from nursing home foley bags that over-dressed people wear
standing fainting with boredom waiting while they write out their checks
even the men have it on

is this the freedom they say the whole world yearns for
two fast-talking guys selling state-of-the-art blowdriers
at closeout prices to a numb-faced clerk

a one-legged man came out of the fog
that crept between the highrises of the financial district
approached the afterwork bus stop for a little change
a hollowed feeling when the heart remembers
the unwritten line here a speechless longing
that can't be described except through the evocation of another
the one who continues up the hill
a pantleg flapping with an empty sound

you might be my own child on this alien street
Pasolini could speak of displaced shepherds in a pastoral of scrapheaps
but I pass you sad confused and mute your vacant mumble and your
bare young neck

that's why nobody's in that seat
because of the smell of him a mineral smell like iron earth
nodding his old head balding with bits of city chaff caught in his hair
that he jerks awake crying am I in an all-night movie
as the bus plunges down into night Chinatown
oh father father father father father

there will be a time
when the world no longer maims us
no I mean they who after picking our pockets
knock us down and kick us in the head
that's why so many of us go along lame
you on one aluminum crutch and one stick picked up
from some waste place walking along in hunger and want
pain and deprivation warping your limbs
if all men were one man he would be you
dragging yourself along you pull us all forward

back and forth every moment up and down this block

blackened feet first sign of gangrene early in the decade

that they were removing me like an old fixture

thin men on Mission St selling their blood

sad Easter-open greasy-spoons

cop strides into the check-cashing joint

everything shoplifted bare as relief

the one arrested with us who cursed and howled for her confiscated bed
was down by the curb in my dream singing so sweetly

we were living down in the subway he said we'd go for walks together along the tracks

he said you can't or don't want to own anything down here but you
can own a cloud

I dreamed that my life was only a short time more and was weeping to lose the simple joys of it hell hosed clean of human tears each dawn

it's the dead who make us kind

from a deep hole those moments of truth a furious grievous weeping
and raging

Born in Chicago in 1946, Sarah Menefee has been writing poetry for over 30 years and has been widely published in journals and magazines such as *Acts, Compages, Channel, Baltimore Sun, People's Tribune, Volition, Left Curve, Real Fiction, Exit Zero, Gas, Working Classics, Worm in the Rain, Deluge, Beatitude,* and *Conjunctions.* She has read her poetry in the San Francisco Bay Area benefits for the homeless movement; and 'guest edits' the art and poetry pages of *Poetry USA.* Her first collection of poetry *I'm Not Thousandfurs* was published by Curbstone Press in 1986.

A member of the Communist Labor Party, Menefee is a correspondent for *The People's Tribune.* As a homeless activist for the past seven years, with the San Francisco Union of the Homeless, Food Not Bombs, and the Homeless Task Force, she has participated in a number of actions and campaigns — including a shelter strike, housing takeovers, a series of civil disobedience actions during police sweeps of homeless encampments, and the 'criminal' sharing of food with the hungry. She was brought to trial in 1991 for feeding the hungry 'without a permit' with the group Food Not Bombs, but after six months of organized public support charges were dropped. Menefee currently resides in San Francisco where she works in a bookstore and continues her work in the cultural and poor peoples' movements.

Related poetry titles from Curbstone Press

THE BOTTOM LINE, poems by Jack Hirschman. The best of Hirschman's work, spanning 10 years, is assembled here in one landmark volume. "*The Bottom Line* is a clear design for the work of a people's poet. Hirschman is tender but tough, with a steel fist in his velvet glove." — *San Francisco Chronicle*. $9.95pa. 0-915306-73-5.

THE CONCRETE RIVER, poems by Luis J. Rodriguez. "For Rodriguez, poetry is a sacred act that can rescue the poet's past in order to instruct his community about his relationship to it and the world." — *The American Book Review*. Winner of the 1991 PEN/Josephine Miles Award. $9.95pa. 0-915306-42-5.

ENDLESS THRESHOLD, poems by Jack Hirschman. This is a people's poetry, a poetry that makes the suffering and resistance of many the believable essence of life in the US today. "These poems engage the reader on every page....the refreshingly nonacademic quality will attract new readers to poetry." — *Library Journal*. $10.95pa. 1-880684-00-4.

I'M NOT THOUSANDFURS, poems by Sarah Menefee. These poems give voice to the lives of the oppressed and exploited everywhere. "Menefee is a genuine item." — *Choice*. "A complex and interesting first collection." — *Small Press*. $6.00pa. 0-915306-59-X.

MEMORY SAYS YES, poems by Margaret Randall. "Margaret Randall is among those most enduring artists who choose/dare to express political sensibility in poetry of the heart." — Holly Near. $7.95pa. 0-915306-77-8.

REBELLION IS THE CIRCLE OF A LOVER'S HANDS, poems by Martín Espada. The third volume of poetry by this widely acclaimed poet. "Astonishingly bold young poet." — *New York Times Book Review*. Winner of the 1989 PEN/Revson Award and the 1991 Paterson Poetry Prize. $9.95PA. 0-915306-95-6.

THE SEA OF TRANQUILITY, poems by Don Gordon. "Don Gordon is one of the most overlooked poets of the 20th century, and the publication of this book is a great service to the...poetry community." — *Bloomsbury Review*. $5.95pa. 0-915306-79-4.

FOR A COMPLETE CATALOG, SEND YOUR REQUEST TO:
Curbstone Press, 321 Jackson Street, Willimantic, CT 06226